Copyright © 2018 by Shanya Price. All rights reserved. This book or any portion thereof may not be reproduced or used in any manner whatsoever without the express written permission of the publisher except for the use of brief quotations in a book review. Printed in the United States of America.

To my dad, who paused everything to watch me become the woman I am today. May you receive all you've waited for throughout your brand-new journey.

To all of the people who supported me and contributed to the completion of this book.

PART I

The First Step

Starting over is something that everyone thinks about but doesn't always have the courage to do. Whether it's a new relationship, a big move, or a change in your life that's unexpected, it can rock your world. Whether planned or forced, it's usually met with some kind of anxiousness, which takes away its appeal. This anxiousness turns people off because it's a sign of being beyond our comfort zone.

> *I don't feel like I started over. I just feel like I kept going. Maybe you don't realize it until it's over and you look back. I don't know if you ever know that you're starting over when you start.*
>
> —Erin A

Starting over is as wonderful as it is terrifying. When people feel that push or pull that tells them to move forward, it's often met with an extreme amount of work. You work hard to find the pieces that were missing before the journey began. Sometimes, you may not know that something is missing, but when you get to the other side, you see how the journey made you stronger.

How did I start over?

I cried and laughed. I pushed myself out of bed when I felt like crap. It was extremely hard and seemed impossible, but I knew that, on the other side, I would thank myself for those moments.

What is there to lose by starting over?

Oftentimes, people are afraid to start over because they believe that they'll lose the life they have—that they'll lose something valuable. If you're starting over at a new job, you're not losing everything you learned at the previous job. You may not see it now, but what you did at the previous job in some way prepared you for the next position you will have. While you're focusing on what was left behind, you're missing out on new lessons you could be learning.

Even if you didn't intend on overthinking what led up to this point, it's likely to happen. If it was the loss of a loved one, did you lose the memories of your time together? Use those times to push you forward. All of the gems they gave you before they passed serve a purpose.

Diligence is to work as food is for the body.

—Nya P

Sometimes people would rather stay in a situation that is toxic for them than start at the beginning stages of something new. Staying hidden can seem more appealing than revealing where things went wrong and owning your part in it so you can move on. The truth? You're really hurting yourself in the long run. Starting over can be embarrassing, but it's a part of life.

It's quite an extraordinary journey to find yourself in, especially after heartbreak, loss, shame, or guilt of any kind. Feeling like you have failed at something you may have wanted with your whole heart can be a lot to deal with, so how *do* you start over? How do you regain the peace and joy that may have been robbed from you? How do you move on from something you were so sure would work?

I searched myself; I cried, prayed, and sought solace in my family and friends, but I continued to feel that something was missing. I honestly still do sometimes. I wanted to hear how other people dealt with situations that caused them to change course. At one point, starting over seemed impossible to me. I felt incompetent at work; my relationship began to crumble; and I barely knew how to navigate where I was in that moment.

Beginning adulthood as a first-generation college student meant that I had to figure some things out on my own. I had no clue about how to accurately manage my money because I hadn't been exposed to many financially literate people. People assume that things are easy for me because of how much I've grown, but starting over in most cases is very difficult. Through wins and losses, adjustments always need to be made.

So the journey of writing this book began for me. I reached out to family, friends, colleagues, and old classmates, so they could share their "start-over stories." As the responses came in, I realized that everyone has their own special way of picking themselves up and starting fresh. Within each story, you'll find unique responses to the question I asked.

I wholeheartedly believe that reading the accounts contained in this book will inspire you. If you've ever had to start over, go back to square one, or create a new beginning in your life, you are *not* alone.

Be patient when starting over. Things may not pick up right away, but they're bound to come together in due time. You'll see why your path had to change. Slowly but surely, you'll regain that pep in your step; the smile you thought you'd lost will return; and at last, your heart will heal.

My Start-Over Story

I had to start over after five years of being in a relationship. Over time, we tried to make it work but always ended up frustrated. I decided to love on purpose and was hurt by the fact that the love I gave wasn't exactly returned.

It took me to a state of depression. I overindulged in alcohol and did almost everything except face the reality of what was happening. I was losing myself, trying to keep someone who didn't care to be kept. When I finally packed my bags, though, I felt a freedom that I haven't felt in ages. I wasn't worried about being cheated on or family issues.

I'm honestly just starting over, and this journey is incredibly difficult at times. I'm super excited for what

God will give me, and other times, I'm a ball of nerves. This doesn't feel real at all, and I question it but not God.

Take your time. Cry if you need to. Surround yourself with people who love you and will encourage you to move forward. Laugh every chance you get. Be strong because even though it's hard right now, it won't always be like this. The truth is that starting over can suck. It causes you to dig deep within yourself and pull out things that no longer serve a purpose in your life. You will cry, and you will be unsure, but it's worth it.

Sometimes, the pain can seem like it's too much to bear. It can be a lot to deal with, and you may feel like giving up, but please don't quit. There's a fighter within you that will emerge throughout the process. Truthfully,

I used to believe that if you want to do something, you should just do it, and I remember hearing all the time that it's a process. Starting over is a process that starts within the mind. You have to change your mindset and believe that what you want is possible for you. Once you begin to believe in your abilities, you'll take the first steps toward becoming the person you want to be. Take one step at a time; research information about the career move you want to make; visit a new state or create a one-year plan. Then, move on to bigger steps that will help you move closer to your goal. Lastly, stay consistent and dedicated to the goals you set, and you'll gradually move forward.

Don't feel like you have to rush for *anyone*. Your journey is YOURS and yours alone. Some people take longer to process their thoughts and ideas—and to act on them—than others. It's normal to have moments of uncertainty. It's normal to be unsure about where you're heading, but DO NOT STAY WHERE YOU ARE. Sorry to yell it but, I cannot stress this enough. DO NOT STAY IN YOUR VALLEY. Take a chance. Assess what's required for success, and adjust to fit where your life is headed. Seek God. Seek and listen to your conscience.

One thing I've realized while transitioning from China back to America is that God will always protect you. I've done some pretty stupid things while being away, and I'm still alive, well, and I'm better than when I came here. So, what are you afraid of? Life will take its course whether you stay stagnate or step out and follow your dreams. Do you really want to live life saying that you didn't even try to love again, start that business, go to school, buy a house, or attempt whatever dream or vision you have in your spirit?

I don't know about you, but I don't plan on sitting around and watching life pass me by without even trying to reach the goals I set for myself. What I've learned about starting over is that it can be all-consuming, it takes up your mind, and you have no choice but to acknowledge that things will never be the same. You realize that you can't continue doing things the same way you were doing them before. Something has to change. You know what starting over really is?

Elevation.

This is amazing to me!

I'm a teacher and a researcher, so I had to look at the proper definition of elevation.

Elevation – *an act or result of lifting or raising someone* or something

- We charted the *elevations* in her temperature.
- His *elevation* to (the position of) chairman was a surprise to many.

I honestly haven't met many people who have gone through a situation that caused them to switch courses that didn't come out with at least a higher level of thinking. So, think about your situations, past or present, this way: What you deem punishment may really be a promotion, as your previous level of life was just a bridge of progression. You have to transition over that bridge to reach the promotion. What a joy it is to know that we won't remain where we began.

The researcher in me had to look up *start* and *over*, so here are the definitions:

Start - *to begin a course or journey*

Over - *in an upward and forward direction across something*

Put those two words together, and what do you get?

When you start over, you begin a journey that takes you in an upward direction. What does that equal?

If you guess *elevation,* you're right, honey! It's so important that this sticks in your head!

Starting over = elevation!

Once this is locked in your brain, starting over for

any reason will become personal in a positive way. You'll shift away from "Why me?" to "What's next for me?" You may not understand why this is happening, but you'll know where your journey is going to take you—UPWARD! That's right. Even if it doesn't give you riches, it will enhance you in some way. You may grow by way of wisdom, networking opportunities, joy, or peace. Whatever the case, this will only serve you throughout your progression.

All of the people who decided to share their stories have grown in some way from what causes them to start over. They have a strength that was designed uniquely for them. What is this strength attached to? To their *purpose*, of course!

Some of these accounts were out of their control, and they had no choice but to learn how to live without a loved one they lost. They had to draw their unique strength so they could grow from their situation and not let it control their life.

How amazing is it what we go through—how amazing that the times we've experienced in starting over, whether voluntary or involuntarily, can be used to help comfort us! There is a healing that comes from reckoning with a past or even a present situation that you were ignoring. There is a peace that comes with knowing that once you start a transition and start over, your journey can only take you up.

This only works if you start. You have to start your journey to move over (upward direction) to get to your next level of elevation, which is your promotion. Your purpose is tied to every level of progression that you will transition through. Just as you use a bridge to get to another city, you have to use the bridge of transition to reach the promotion that's waiting for you.

Again, I repeat this only happens if YOU start!

The next part of this book is composed of real stories from real people, recounting the process of starting over. The people who volunteered to share their stories come from all walks of life and vary in age and ethnicity.

As people who are drawn to emotions, we can be pulled into our feelings and believe that no one could possibly understand how we feel. I think at some point in our lives, we've all felt this way. This is my favorite part of the book because I or someone I know can relate to each story here. It makes me feel less alone in my own personal journey.

Y'all this is some good stuff!

You never know what people are dealing with when you're looking at their beautiful faces! They could be hiding sickness, heartache, loss defeat, depression, and any number of painful emotions behind that smile you see at work, school, or on the street.

Everyone is fighting their own battle, and even the strongest soldiers need to feel like they have someone who understands—or at least sympathizes with—what they're going through.

It's my hope that this helps you in whatever state you're in. Whether you're strong, weak, joyful, or discontent, I pray you find some solace in the fact that other people have made it out of their respective situations or are still working their way through them and fighting with all of their might.

I asked these four questions to myself and all of the participants before you continue to think about them and reflect on your situation . . .

Describe a time when you had to start over in a specific area of your life.

How did starting over impact your life positively or negatively?

If you're just starting over, explain your thoughts on your journey so far.

What advice or thoughts can you share about starting over to someone who is reluctant or scared to take the first step?

PART II

How Did I Start Over? Stories . . .

Starting Over After Marriage

I had to start over after my wife and I divorced, so I guess that would fall under the personal/relationship umbrella. It's one of the hardest things I've ever had to do.

It impacted me negatively because it caused me to question everybody's motives. I'm always suspicious of people's real intentions and why they're really interacting with me. But the one positive thing that happened was that I regained my independence. I found my drive again. Now that I'm single, I know what I want, and I also know what I will or won't put up with.

At first, I thought this was the hardest, most miserable, most time-consuming thing I've ever done in my life. I've had good times where I've met amazing people and have done things I've never thought I'd do. I've learned what I'm really capable of. I've had bad times where I felt like I wasn't good enough for anybody and suicidal thoughts crept into the back of my head. But so far, I don't regret starting over because I feel like I've become a better person.

My advice for anyone about to start over is to simply make the leap before you can talk yourself out of it. Don't hesitate. It's going to be scary. It's going to be uncomfortable. And it's going to take you out of your comfort zone. But, if you make it out the other side, you'll be a stronger, better person in the end.

Moving to Start Over ...

Shanya! This is beautiful. I periodically see your posts on Facebook, and it always warms my heart to know you're doing well and are always willing to shine in this world. It's a trick of living that I think I'm only just beginning to fully own ... You have had it for a long time now.

Your book sounds inspiring, and it's just what people need right now. Sometimes, letting go and stepping foot on a new path full of unknowns is one of the hardest things we can do. When you take that step, it can be scary as hell or sometimes the only way forward because you've hammered the "normal" path into oblivion ...

I accidentally moved to Maui after doing my second yoga training here. I wasn't fully conscious of how much my shifts would change my life . . . but if I had been, I think it would have been much harder. All I knew was that I needed to stay in this beautiful place with all these wonderful people I had met so that I could slow down and re-evaluate my life. I wasn't happy and wasn't willing to sacrifice happiness for society anymore.

Now . . . five years later, I'm still here, and we have started a little farm. There are still major ups and downs that come with trotting into the unknown, but now . . . I'm creating from the heart. It's my truest wish to farm and research regenerative agriculture. The energy that comes from following this path is **IMMENSE!**

I'll share more when I have a moment to write it cohesively. Right now . . . I'm just gushing excitement because the day is Heaven; I just made fresh bread, and I got this inspiring message from a wonderful woman! I'm sending you lots of love and light. Thank you for thinking of me. This work is sure to be a gift to the world.

Musically Starting Over . . .

Every time I feel like I'm losing my reach with my music, I feel like I have to start over with different methods to regain that reach. Every time I feel that way, the starting over periods make me feel inadequate. It can be a negative impact because I choose to allow my emotions to get in the way of my purpose. That said, I feel like I'm getting closer every time I do start over.

Never be afraid to start over. Things can be done differently, and you learn each time you try something new. Time isn't wasted unless that time isn't used to get you in the right direction. Just because you have to start over doesn't mean the time you spent on what you *thought* would work for you amounts to wasted time.

Starting Over and Forgiving God

I had to start over in life when I lost my mother. I was so lost and mad at God for taking away my mom. I was depressed and hurt and upset, and at the same time, I wanted to die. I didn't care that I'd lost my care for life and everything in it. I became so bitter and hurt that I didn't care if I died or lived. I wanted to die every day I lost my motivation in life, and I hated GOD. I didn't even want to hear the word GOD, and it got so bad that I was truly losing my mind.

Now years have passed, and I'm trying to rebuild my relationship with God and live a life that's for Him. This is the first time in my life that I have actually trusted God, and now I'm living a life that is positive and true and doing what I have to do. My advice is to never give up your trust in God—and enjoy life to the fullest no matter what.

Starting Over for Improvement

So, I think that life is actually a series of starting over. I teach, so every year I get a chance to start over. I learn from my previous mistakes, see what works and what doesn't, and get to improve myself and my instruction.

One way I guess I started over is when I was laid off from my favorite job in the nonprofit sector. I knew I had to make myself more marketable. I had worked in mental health with children for eight years and then in college and career counseling for three. So, I returned for a second master's (my first is in nonprofit org) and worked toward my education degree. I knew I needed it to find and keep employment. And I'm technically in a transition period, ready to start over now. I'm relocating to Beijing to teach science. New country, new school, new apartment, new language. Starting over is an opportunity to run with what you did well and learn from what you did wrong.

I feel that starting over is nothing to be reluctant about. It's a fresh way to see life, career, and family. It's a way to strike out and be someone new. A way to right your wrongs. And yes, when starting over, you'll make mistakes, but those mistakes help you grow. Sure, starting over is scary, but if you don't move forward or do something new, you'll never know what great thing lies directly ahead of you.

Starting Over without Regret

Girl, I feel like I'm *always* starting over. Sometimes by choice and other times not so much. My first big start-over was when I moved to Spain. I had to break up with a toxic boyfriend, which meant I had to change schools regardless of what I wanted . . . so, I made the move, and it was the best decision I ever made. New life, new world, new friends, new path.

My mom suddenly had a stroke and I left Madrid within hours—with little more than the clothes on my back. I didn't think I would end up staying, but it seemed to be way more serious than I thought. I left my clothes, books, pictures, friends, sexy men, sexy apartment, and dream job behind to be with my mama.

Again, I will never regret that decision. I would choose it a hundred times. But not getting to say goodbye and not packing up my apartment myself left me depressed and broken for a long time.

After my mom was better and able to be on her own, I had to get out and be me again. I moved to China. Again, it proved a good move. It may not have been as carefree and amazing as my first adventure, but nothing ever is. It's different here, and as an LLD, it's difficult to make friends sometimes—especially within your own center. I've made some friends . . . some not-exactly-friends—ha-ha—and now a husband, which trumps all. He is my everything, and we're about to have our first baby.

The next change is in the works. Now that I'm not in the center, I'm finding myself trying to make a change. I didn't choose to leave my center, which leaves me a bit broken like before in Spain, but I have the power to remember the good and bad from that and try and make the most of it. I have reached out on FB to find new friends, new social circles, new everything. Only time shall tell because the next change will be motherhood, which will be a lifelong adventure

I know you're finishing up here and starting over. The best advice I can give you is to make every second count because you don't know when it will be taken away. When changes do occur that are out of your control, find ways to adjust and make it work for you. There's always a silver lining, so remember the good and the bad. This too shall pass, so make it good. Good luck with your life change, lady!

Leaving a Toxic Relationship to Start Over

I started over in 1994, when I decided to leave a stagnant relationship in New York. I had three little kids and my parents had retired and moved to Virginia leaving me the home. My then-boyfriend told my dad he was planning on marrying me and providing for our soon-to-be family. Well, he never moved in nor did he help support us. I started to realize I was a booty call to him. I was ashamed that that was all I was to him. His parents wouldn't help because they didn't want to get involved. Then, I broke my leg and my youngest was in the hospital, and his dad refused to stay at the hospital with him while I stayed home with the other two kids and a broken leg.

At that moment, I thought, *Am I this desperate for a man who is doing nothing for me?* Then, his own father told me his son is not a man until he does right by me and the kids. He also said if he doesn't respect them, then I don't stand a chance. So, I called my sister that night in Maryland and told her I needed to leave. That next morning, she and her husband came and rented a U-Haul, and I took what I could, and I left to never return. It was hard starting over. I cried a lot but thanked God more. I don't regret my children but I regret not being strong enough to leave sooner.

Being with someone who makes you feel less than worthy of their commitment to you is no way to leave. I would walk with my head down. I would struggle to make ends meet, and I would lie to my parents, telling them everything was great when I was actually living in hell. I felt like I was in a pit trying to claw my way out. However, I thank God for allowing me to go through what you have been through because it made me strong enough to deal with the next few things that happened in my life.

Learning a lesson While Starting Over

I had to start over at the age of twenty-two. I'd been living with my significant other since the age of seventeen and learned that, during this time, I was being cheated on—and it wasn't with just one other woman. This was at a time I was just finishing high school, entering college, providing for him and myself, etc.

This had a positive and negative impact on my life. I had to start over and also began questioning my appearance, but after a while, I received positive feedback from others, and it boosted my confidence. My advice would be to take everything as a lesson. I understand that there's a reason and a season for everything.

Acknowledging the Need to Start Over

A time I had to start over in my life was when I had a severe mental and emotional breakdown in 2013 in the middle of class. Everything that I had been holding in from my mom's passing, my current relationship break up at the time, and the stress of school weighed down on me all at once. I started crying hysterically in the middle of class while hyperventilating.

I was escorted to the counseling center, where I talked for hours to someone and literally had to reset everything. It was hard. I was at my lowest point, and I didn't know what to do. From that day on, I knew I had to simply start over and take it one day at a time to heal myself. It's still an ongoing process, but I've recovered, and I'm thankful that I had a chance to start over again. And I realize that it's okay to not be okay and to just start over and grow again.

Starting over impacted my life more positively than negatively. It gave me a chance to really look deep within myself and face my depression, which had been eating away at me for years. It was hard at first, but eventually, it became easier to get through each day. Initially, the negative impact was my failure to eat and practice proper hygiene for a while because I was still facing myself and trying to forgive people. Trying to come to an understanding that I'd lost my mom was so hard. But day by day, the negatives turned to positives, and it was easier to get through the days.

I've been starting over for years now, and I've really come far, though there are days where I relapse and go into a bad place. But I'm able to get out of them and move on and continue to grow. It's a never-ending process for me, but I take pride in knowing that I've come so far and I'm continuing to go far.

Advice that I would give about starting over would be that it's okay not to be okay and that you can go at your own pace. Some days will get really hard and others won't, but just know that you can get through it. And it's okay to cry and have off days. Take time to get yourself back to a stable condition. Nobody is forcing you to get better faster because everyone has their own pace at which they deal with things. Most importantly, regard yourself with love and kindness. Take care of your soul

and know that you can do it even when it's tough.

Learning About Yourself While Starting Over

My mother NEVER got sick—not even a cold! We lived together for forty-two years, minus when I went away to school. When I bought her a house in 2000, we moved from the one she'd been renting. In 2009, I found out she needed a lung transplant, so I stopped working to care for her. Almost four years later, she died. I lost my home, lost my job, and had two children to care for. Starting over impacted me negatively, as I hadn't prepared for life without her. I was consumed by caring for her, and after her death, I had so much debt to dig myself out from under. Starting over impacted me positively because, after her death, the life I had planned for my children (which was put on hold for many, many years) finally came back into focus, and I began to work very hard toward it. I moved to Upper Darby and am still building!

I'm starting over in a new township, and it's a bit lonely but not scary. I'm out here and all of my family is scattered throughout Philly, but I have about four close friends who are a great support system and drop by often. I'm very busy with my daughter's dance, acting, modeling, work, and ministry, so when we do come home . . . we crash. LOL.

It's a good journey because I'm in a great place in my life (rediscovering who I am and what I like and want). My advice to someone reluctant or scared to start over is to pray first (I asked God for wisdom and direction). I made a vision board (including what I want for the second half of my life), and I bought a whole new wardrobe—and new furniture. I began to look at each new day as "I'm so worth it all! I'm worth the fight!"

Problems are a part of life, so learn from them (if only to know what you don't want and what NOT to do again). Be willing to take a risk! Laugh a lot more than you used to, and don't take yourself or others too seriously. Give yourself room to make mistakes (stop being a perfectionist). Most importantly, enjoy the journey on your way to the purpose (your destination)!!!

Academically Starting Over

I had to start over several times in college. I didn't know what I wanted to major in; I thought it was music when I first got there, so I did a full four years, but that wasn't working, so I started over, went to the early education department, started on my track there, and met my future wife. Education didn't work out either, but it all worked out in the end. I majored in psychology, graduated with a 3.9, and got engaged to the love of my life. Trust the process, as God knows best. Don't mind the start-over; it's always for the good.

Going Through the Process of Starting Over

My career. Since I was a little girl, I envisioned being an architect. I went to school, with a few years of not being financially cleared, and God somehow worked it out. I completed my degree, graduated with honors, and was feeling excited about working in the field. After graduating, I found it beyond complicated to get a job practicing in my field. Four years of working as a teacher, teaching something I desired to practice, hurt. The first few years I tried to maintain optimism, saying to myself, "God's going to work it out; the right opportunity is on its way."

I watched classmates that never really shared my passion get multiple opportunities, then quit because they wanted to. It amazed me. After enough time, (in my eyes) of getting that thrown in my face and continuing to work in a career I never wanted, I worked up the courage to let go of the cushion of teaching, with the hope that God would provide the perfect career opportunity. After taking that leap and hitting the ground yet again, I began to resent God; I began to lose trust in Him. I started to grow bitter. For months and months, I tried to win this battle over the flesh and revitalize my mind to accept God's word as truth. But the bitterness continued to feed on my heart. After many nights of the tug and pull, I cried out to Him.

Starting over spiritually and revamping my relationship with God turned my life around. I began to regain confidence in myself and began updating my resume to try again. A day before I was getting ready to send my resume off to a list of architectural firms, I received an email asking me to come in for a second interview for the architectural firm that I actually interviewed with a year ago. It was also the first firm on my list. I nailed the interview and was hired the same day.

It's amazing how much we, as people and even Christians rely, so much on ourselves to get things done. We have to trust the process. The birth of the new situation, position, new status, and new you is appreciated more, and your drive to maintain and even enhance your abilities is strengthened. We don't always have the answers nor can we see what God sees. The human in us can get in God's way.

I can't say it enough: trust the process! It may seem impossible, drawn-out, overwhelming, depressing, and even hard to accept, but if you truly believe God wants nothing but the best for you, then you can't fail. But you have to do your part, and a huge chunk of your part is accepting God's words as truth and having an incredible faith that even the most persistent dark days couldn't intervene. Something that simple can change any situation.

To People Reluctant to Start Over

Upon graduation, I was unable to seal the deal by failing my summer class. Not only did I find myself in a jam, but I found myself having to rebuild who I was and what I wanted to do with my life. I had to ask myself who am I? What do I stand for? What am I passionate about? What can I not go without doing for myself and others?

I no longer saw myself in the career path I was taking. I had to start over by not only rebuilding my foundation but my support system and confidence in myself. My career choice and my self-identity were always one and the same to me. So, when I lost sight of my place in the career world, I had to rediscover myself.

It's nothing like choosing to give yourself a clean slate even when no one else is willing to. The positive impact of starting over is allowing yourself to grow in ways unimaginable; doors will open that you didn't know existed before, and your mind will continuously broaden in perspective and understanding. Life is what we make it. If we chose to strive with a positive thriving mindset, then we'll prosper in our lives. So, take the good with what seems like the bad but understand those are just lows and learning opportunities for growth.

Taking the time to reevaluate my life's work and career choice is a challenge I chose to conquer every day. It's been an overall positive journey but naturally, there are low points. The lows come when things get hard and you just wish you could rush the process. Sometimes, I find myself contemplating my decisions and wondering if being complacent about my life would be better. Then, I ask myself, *Am I happy? Will I grow the way I would like to?*

So far, the journey has been absolutely amazing, but it's a ride nonetheless. There are the upbeat times and the lows too. But I ask myself where would I'd be had I not made the decision to start over. Probably somewhere I don't want to imagine. I just have to remain confident about my decision and understand that everything happens for a reason. Second chances are a blessing and with every blessing, there is a lesson. I'm just an eager student ready to continuously learn about myself and find my place in the world.

The advice I would share with someone who is reluctant to start over? I would simply say this: cast your fears aside, forget about what could go wrong, and just do it. We'll never know how far we can go until we decide to move forward. Don't stagnate yourself by remaining stuck in time or space. Take a moment to be still and think about which direction you would like to go today. Starting over is a journey, but the first step of the journey is realizing there is a new path waiting for you to take. Hold onto your truths and what drives you and the journey will be an amazing one.

Starting Over in a Relationship

At the age of nineteen, I got pregnant and wasn't married. I was only two semesters away from completing my undergraduate degree. I felt defective and guilty. I felt like I had failed my entire family. I felt like I was continuing the cycle of the women before me that never reached their dreams. The cycle of brokenness in the family structure and values. As a young girl, I wanted to be the change in our family structure because it would help our future generations. I dreamt of becoming the first to graduate with a four-year degree. To get married to a man I loved and raise a family in a traditional way. I used to look at the television show *Leave it to Beaver* and imagine my family seated at the dinner table communing with one another.

We would look at pictures of our vacations and discuss our future plans. We would share our dreams and encourage one another to become all that God created us to be. We would feel loved and give love freely.

After my boyfriend's initial response, I felt those dreams shatter into tiny pieces. He was young and we were both in college. We weren't being responsible, so as a result, we got pregnant and our plans changed. It was a shocker for both of us. We both felt guilty that this beautiful miracle was now associated with unpleasant emotions. Prior to getting pregnant, we talked about marriage and what it would be like, but we hadn't set a date. We were playing around with the idea. We started looking at rings, and then I believe my boyfriend got cold feet. I later found out that he was in shock that I wanted a ring that cost $5000, which he could barely afford with his part-time job.

He was afraid that he couldn't take care of me, so he avoided the idea after that trip to the mall. I was so confused because he never shared this with me until later. Shortly after that, I noticed that our relationship was different. It wasn't positive. I began to feel like he wasn't the right one, but then I found out I was pregnant. Feeling unsure of our future, I began to prepare for the cycle I dreaded for my family but I was going to make sure my daughter felt loved. I remember going to places, and they would ask do you have a husband? I would say no, and the looks of judgment would make me feel ashamed.

My boyfriend and I continued to date. Around seven months into my pregnancy, he asked me to marry him in front of forty family members. I said yes! But deep down in my soul, I wasn't sure we were ready for this kind of commitment. I explained to him my dream of a traditional family and he said that was what he wanted as well. I asked him to give us thirteen months of engagement to be sure that we were committed to this union.

To say it was easy would be misleading you. It has been a journey. I would say that what I learned through this process is that everything in life happens for a reason. Having our daughter was a shocker because I was told I couldn't have children at the age of fourteen, but God had different plans. After having our son, I had to have a hysterectomy at the age of thirty, so I can no longer have children.

We have two beautiful children together, and we love them dearly. We enjoy family time together. We cook and eat together. We play board games and watch movies together. We share our dreams and goals. We encourage one another to achieve our goals. My family was right there when I achieved my master's degree and started my Mary Kay business. They have been there through it all. My husband and I sit back at times and think about how far we have come. We often say that with God on our side, we can never fail. We make sure that God is the head of our relationship together and individually. We believe that is the secret to having a healthy marriage and family. It's worked for us for over twenty years, and our biggest goal is to celebrate seventy-five years of marriage, healthy and whole together. Now that is a plan I'm looking forward to sharing with all of you.

Thoughts on Starting Over

From the outside, I think starting over and sticking to what a person believes in has a positive impact on life. The person is able to see clearly in difficult situations and able to have a different outlook. Because I haven't really had to start over, I don't have a personal account to share.

Starting over isn't easy for anyone—especially starting over alone. I would say that one should confide in a trustworthy person to tell them what the situation is and ask for support throughout the journey that is about to be taken. Also, because I have strong faith-based values, I would say that one should put their trust in the Lord. Sometimes, starting fresh gives new perspectives on life. You are destined for greatness, and at times, one may steer off the path that God has set for us, and starting over is the best option. Let go, and watch God move.

Starting Over After the Loss of a Child

I'm now embarking on my new life as a childless mother. The challenges of starting over are at a standstill. The numbness of being without the only child that grew inside of me is crippling, preventing me from being 100% committed to the journey I know I have to walk. Starting over, for me, seems to be so far out of my reach right now. The good part about it is, I know in my heart that it's coming.

This impact has gone both ways. Despite the pain I continue to endure, I know I'm in my own way moving forward with the renewal, exposed to how much love and blessing God has bestowed upon me.

So far, I have maintained my happiness in the public eye. I still struggle with secretive depression on the inside.

Try not (I know it's easier said than done) to overwhelm yourself with agenda items that aren't attainable. Be upfront and honest about what you can and cannot do. Make time for yourself! That has to be the most important of all. One of the many things I'm learning about starting over is that you have to learn who you are all over again.

Take Your Time, Stay Positive, and Start Over!

I transferred from Hampton University to the University of Memphis in my senior year of college. I created a plan to be successful and stayed the course. I got the best grades, and I was the most focused after taking a semester off of school.

Starting over impacted me positively because I realized then that I could truly accomplish any task I was committed to. I worked hard to secure internships in my field and go after other opportunities to market myself as the best candidate for entry-level positions.

As a human, our mental capacity affords us the ability to do anything that our minds consider a viable option. Even though that sounds like a cliché, it's so true. Surround yourself with positive people and focus on your end goal. Create a plan to attain that goal, and evaluate your progress following a personal timeline. You determine the pace of your success by the energy that you put forth. Nothing is impossible, but you have to work diligently for the things that you want in life.

Starting Over Abroad

In 2010, I graduated with my Bachelor of Education Degree, taught as a trained teacher for the first time, and got accepted into the Master of Arts in Counseling Program at Hampton University. It was a very big year for me, to say the least. I had to move my entire life to a new country, and that was stressful. Having to gather documentation to get my student visa granted and not knowing all of the steps that I needed to take took a toll on me and discouraged me a bit. After getting to Hampton and meeting my professors, I found out that my two-year program was actually a three-year program, and that only heightened my anxiety.

My first semester was rough. I was in a two-bedroom apartment with three other girls, one of whom was my cousin. They were all beautiful and amazing young women, but we all had different personalities, and I had never mastered the art of living with others. On top of that, my great-grandmother passed away at the age of 101. All I wanted to do was go back home. But I didn't. In the spring of 2011, I moved onto campus and shared a room with a young lady who has become one of my closest friends (we still keep in touch). I had gotten a car by this point and didn't have to depend on people as much, so my anxieties began to melt away. I had a family through my major and a family through the HU Gospel Choir, several of whom I'm still friends with, and though I've had random obstacles along the way, I'm glad I made the decision to attend Hampton University.

I may now have a chance to start over all over again in another country, and if I'm able to, I'm going to take it! If you have the opportunity to start over, embrace it. If you're anything like me, it's going to be scary because you'll be stepping out into the unknown. You may be going to a place where you have no friends or family members, and the idea of being alone and possibly lonely may give you a knot in your stomach. That's okay! Take the chance, anyway.

Hold strong to the beliefs that you have, as they will help to comfort you. Make new friends who share your beliefs and who add to your life. They'll be the ones you can depend on when times get a little rough. Adopt an adventure mindset, and explore the newness that life will have to offer you in the form of having to start over.

You deserve amazing experiences in your life!

Be Strong and Start Over

I had two simultaneous start-overs that relate to each other. At the start of my graduate year, at the end of September, I experienced a shock when my maternal grandmother passed away. This was a huge hit due to the fact that she was an anchor and pillar in my family. She helped raise my sister and me from our births and was a continuous cheerleader in our corner. After she passed, I had to start over. I had to discover what life looked like without that guidance, personal cheerleader, and strong pillar around anymore.

I sunk into a great depression that only close friends could really notice. Though depressed, I continued forward and started the steep climb out. I began painting and expressing my pain and hurt through artwork and made quite a few pieces. Honestly, it was enough to fill my entire townhouse. Upon graduation, I thought that this climb was over but soon realized that this was only the beginning. After Graduation, having received my Master's Degree, I was jobless and working as a freelance graphic designer at home with my family.

The struggles I had faced trying to get out of my depression had only hardened my heart and spirit to interactions with others, and it became apparent with my interactions with my family. Yet, I believe that everything happens for a reason. Throughout that year and a half, I found myself again. I found my *true* self. I grew closer to my family. I grew closer to myself, and shortly after my realization, I had not one but two job offers. Having accepted the ideal position, I'm still loving and growing to this day.

The experience of my grandmother's passing had a negative impact. It exposed my weakness at a time when I needed to be strong. Yet, coming from the ashes of my pain and depression and being jobless for over a year, I discovered who I was and achieved many life accomplishments, growing in maturity and understanding. Like I said before, I believe that everything happens for a reason.

While I wish that my Grandmother was still around, I know that it was necessary for me to understand that, in life, you have no control over who lives, who dies, or who tells your story. If I could rewrite this history, I would but I wouldn't as well simply because I found who I was truly meant to be.

For anyone that's starting over by choice or by force, remember that life is not meant to be stagnant. We must have changes and shifts in order to find our best selves. No matter the difficulty, no matter the struggles, no matter the hard work and pain you will have to go through, if it's there, press on. It's okay if you have setbacks. Stepping back as an artist allows you to see the whole picture before pressing forward. Don't get too lost in the details that you forget the whole painting. Finally, you are the writer of our own story. Everyone else is a critic and will only have opinions, but as long as you are happy with your work, nothing else should matter.

Know Your Worth and Start Over

I once fell in love with no commitment. As crazy as it sounds, I knew that we would be together. I was good enough. I deserved it. I waited a year and a half . . . emotions a wreck, feelings growing stronger. I waited. And he chose every other woman but me. He kept me close enough not to leave but far enough away to never be seen. It took me looking up at him from the ground to realize I needed—that I was WORTH so much—more. I cried all summer, but afterward, I found myself. I fell in love with myself. I lost my ability to trust anyone. Men could tell me anything they wanted to; I would just smile and nod, believing none of it. I jumped to conclusions at the first sign of offense from any new guy. I vowed to never allow myself to be treated as less than what I was worth.

I made a commitment to only seek God's best for myself in all areas of my life. I picked up and I moved on, so I'm not in that position right now. But if I ever were again, I would be stronger within myself to know when it's time for me to leave. When I'm falling out of love with myself and more in love with someone else, I pay more attention to warning signs and stabilize myself emotionally so that I don't have to feel that pain again. The first step in the process is always the hardest. But take that step. Think enough of yourself to move forward—toward your destiny. The biggest slap in God's face is staying where we are when he has called us to be somewhere so much greater. Change your thoughts about yourself. Constantly affirm yourself. Take your time. Move slowly if you must . . . but MOVE. Move into the full and satisfying life that is waiting for you.

Learning Humility While Starting Over

I am currently "starting over." My return to Chicago from working in Indianapolis for a year has been humbling, to say the least. Being without work for over a month is taxing, especially for someone who is accustomed to providing for himself. I am in a space where I must depend on God for absolutely everything, which is nerve-wracking for my flesh but so comforting for my spirit. Being a man from humble beginnings, I'm reminded of where I come from in this particular chapter of my life, and I don't want to return there. I know I won't. It's just that as a young man—a millennial to be exact—I can sometimes be rather impatient.

For my flesh, it has a negative impact because I'm not in control. I don't have the power to orchestrate anything. It's humbling to the ego and requires a high level of spiritual dependency upon God, which is what He wants from us all. This transition has required me to self-reflect and self-actualize in ways that I'd never done before. It requires me to face my insecurities, my imperfections, and my demons in order to transition into the new space God will have for me.

As I mentioned earlier, it's humbling beyond comparison. It requires me to relinquish all reigns over my life. It requires me to allow God to inhabit all rooms of my home—not confine Him to the foyer and admire the view. In order to truly go where God requires me to be, I must be broken. I must be humbled. I must be exposed to many aspects of my life I didn't know existed—and some that I have brushed off.

Don't avoid the process. Embrace it. The more you resist, the longer the test will be for you. The longer your process will be. God isn't facetious, controlling, dictatorial, or supercilious. He is stern, but compassionate in all His ways. His works are to perfect you, to mold you into who He has called you to be. Your flesh may resist because it is of this world, but your spirit isn't. In your transition, ask for patience, discernment, and peace despite what your circumstances appear to be. They are insignificant compared to your God. They have no power over your God. Embrace the process. The blessing you are expecting or in search of does not supersede the process. It's the bonus you receive from the blessing of the process.

In The Process of Starting Over

To be honest I'm starting over right now, moving on from a failed relationship changing the school where I'm teaching, and going back to school myself. This time last year, I could have never imagined my life where it is now. I was at my dream school, and I was working through things with the man I thought I would marry. When these changes occurred, I literally thought about death because of the pressure and toll it was taking on me mentally, emotionally, and physically. It has been very uncomfortable, but I have faith that starting over is going to blow my mind in ways I've never imagined. God gives his toughest battles to His strongest people, right?

Negatively, I've endured depression, going two months without pay, and low self-esteem. Positively, my faith has been built up, I've been meeting new positive people, and I've moved away from a toxic environment and person. This is a journey that's been hard, but I know it's built a better, stronger me!

God has you! Don't give up!!! God is in this fight with you!!! It's okay to want to be to yourself sometimes, but if you notice the signs of depression or feel yourself sinking back into a dark place, pray . . . and pray some more. It's possible to pray yourself away from that dark place. Trust me. I've done it!

Starting Over with a Deferred Dream

I recently started over in January of 2016. Actually, the entire year of 2016 was built around starting over while also tying up loose strings of dreams left behind. I decided to leave my fifth college in December of 2015 and head back to the school where I knew I belonged—the one that had always been in my heart. The catch? It was two hours from home and I now had a toddler's wellbeing to consider in all my decisions.

However, I was determined to get my degree in 2016, and it had to be from this school. After lots of perseverance, tears, encouraging words, and reminders, I did exactly that and got the job done in December 2016. Now I'm starting over yet again—a new school, a new degree, and also a new career. While it may not be as overwhelming as my journey in 2016, it's still a new beginning and one that I'm approaching with open arms and great expectancy!

It was truly an overwhelmingly positive experience. It introduced me to new strengths in myself that I didn't even know existed. It also highlighted the fact that my support system would sometimes fall to the wayside. While it challenged me in ways I had never once considered, it also left me with a feeling of invincibility and feeling like I could conquer the world. Who wouldn't want to feel like a real-life superhero, you know?

While I completed one journey, my break was short-lived, in a sense, since I am now preparing to embark on another new journey (or two). I had put this off for some time (trying to figure out life's next steps, regrouping, and enjoying life a bit), but one day, I woke up feeling ready and assured it was time to take the steps necessary to get the next journey going. So far, so good. As with everything in life, everything is starting to fall in place and feel just right. I'm excited.

Just do it! If that feeling or thought keeps nagging at you, and you can't seem to escape it, there's a reason why. Think everything through, make your plan (and possibly a backup and a backup for the backup), and get the job done. You'll feel so much better on the other side of completion. I promise!

Making Moves and Starting Over

For a long time, I was strongly convinced that I could accumulate enough savings with which to develop my own investment(s) and thereby support my family. I believed that I could save $100,000 cash and deposit it into some sort of interest-bearing, dividend-paying bank vehicle. I was heavily influenced by not my father but by men who didn't know that I was an aspiring protégé of theirs—men that had practically bought and developed the inner city of Philadelphia ... men that I'd say I was fortunate enough to work for indirectly.

I was strong-willed and persistent in my efforts, possessing all the qualities of one pursuing economic freedom. I would devote 96–100% of my weekly income to savings; I'd look forward to working hard and staying for overtime; I'd rarely be absent; I had no care for fashion or style; and I sat calmly in the house on days when I could've gone out to have a great time. All I read about was finance, and how much more money I could save each year was all I thought about. The acquisition of my dream ruled me.

I had grown so focused on possessing money that it became a game to me, I remember going to banks to get bills transferred to match existing bills in the series of production. It became similar to a trading card game for me. Eventually, I'd saved $50,000 in twenties, and all the while, this money was in a bag in my coat closet, I began to grow worried about its exposure. After all, I was living with my mother, who like many, didn't possess due respect for financial freedom or an understanding of the sacrifices necessary to obtain it.

To facilitate concealing the money, I'd run bundles of $5000 to the bank to exchange for $100 banknotes. There was some speculation and discomfort in the bankers at first, as this behavior will often indicate illicit activities, but they knew I had been a long-time transactional customer and I had been working for quite a while. In due time, all the twenties were converted to hundred-dollar notes.

It had been four years I'd worked saving the money and stashing it away, and my ambition grew the more I accumulated.

One day, while at work, around 12:30 p.m., I received texts from my mother—texts expressing her anger and unwillingness to be sorry for some action she had taken. At first, I had no idea what she was trying to say, and as a serious worker, I went about my business and decided to call her later, as I hadn't perceived that she was in any real harm.

When the end of the day arrived, I headed out of my workplace to my car, started the engine, and notice weird sounds. Immediately, I drove to AutoZone for an inspection, pulling into the parking lot and shutting off the vehicle before speaking to a consultant. Then, I remembered my mother's messages, so I called her ...

She answered on the first ring. It was as if she had been sitting by the phone the entire time since her texts to me earlier. Before I could say anything, she rushes me with, "I don't care how you feel" and "I don't care; I told you I needed some money," so I instantly realized where she was going, and my heart dropped. I calmly asked her how much she had taken, and she replied "Three"—with attitude. I calmly replied "$300?" in question, and she said, "No. $3,000." My heart fell through my chest to the floor of my '98 Ford Taurus. I swear to God.

I was so hurt. Not because of the loss of money—I was saving that much in 4-5 weeks. I was hurt because I had been a victim of theft, and my own mother did it. I had been violated by the last person I thought would hurt me.

My mother and I never really had the warm relationship a mother and son should have. There were always problems between us—hate from me to her, discomfort from her to me—and things between us didn't really stabilize until I moved out at age twenty-two.

This is when I realized that I had to change.

Do What Works For You and Start Over

Re-watched *all* of *Sex and the City*, reread some of my favorite books, and one day, I decided I had spent enough time in the past and got excited about the unknown wonderful possibilities the future held. It's nice to peruse my goals and basically do whatever I want when I want. But I've been called selfish . . . I like doing things and living my life on my terms.

Give yourself time to heal, but don't let pity and sadness be your "resting place." Feel what you feel, but don't let it get in the way of your life. Be kind to yourself. Do what you need to do to get your head right. Treat yourself the way you want to be treated by others. Make a list of everything you want and want to do (a "bucket list"), and get started.

Sickness Cannot Hold You Back From Starting Over

It was around 2010. I was about ten years in. It started at twenty-one, and I was entering my thirties. Ten years in . . . Trained boxers barely last ten rounds. My opponent was myself—my body. I became well acquainted with my opponent, Lupus, in 2001. I was halfway through my senior year at Bowie State University and about to be a real man now.

I wasn't sweating a job. I had already been told that I was needed as a Black man in the field of education. I'm the one that ran a 4.2-second 40-yard dash. I'm the backflip king from the playground. Mr. Phi Theta Kappa and Mr. Kappa Delta Pi. Life for me was good! My future was bright like high beams in the rearview mirror. Five foot five . . . about a buck twenty-nine. I wasn't hurting, but Lupus put a combo on me.

Disability? My mind was able; my body was not. Hair loss, weight loss ... my mind was at a loss regarding my future. 2008 ... 2009 ... the rounds were ticking by. Would this be my life? This wasn't the life I dreamed for myself. I saw myself, at one time, as an Air Force pilot. As a photographer. I saw myself with a wife, beautiful children, a home, and a Lamborghini (when I was nine years old). But being disabled made me unable to reach any of these.

Disabled meant NOT able. Not able to be the man of my own dreams, let alone the man of any woman's dreams. What was my future going to be now? I lay alone one night, surrounded by darkness— externally ... internally. What was the future for me? As dark and empty as the room in which I lay.

What was my reason to live? To be viewed as sickly? Days after day, dulling the pain and being perceived as lame. I had a plan. The tears began to fill my eyes as much as the anguish and sorrow that filled my mind. Then, I realized that my lifeless body would be discovered by my family. What would they feel? Who would find me first? I recalled our fond memories and the many laughs. Would they be able to remain in this place that they called home happily ever after? Who would be there for my brothers after "Niecy-Ma" and "Jimmy-Pop" were gone?

I'm glad there was a standing eight count. At that moment, I decided on a new beginning. I didn't know what the future held for me. But this was my moment for a new beginning. I left the belt in the drawer, cried some more, and decided to stay in the fight.

Here I am today! For whatever reason, I decided to live. I realized I wasn't just living for me. I was in the fight of my life—the fight *for* my life! I had to fight and not just for me. I still don't know what my future holds or how much longer my future will be. But right now I'm able. I'm able and willing to live. I've started over—a new round. I've got to continue the fight.

Learning to Live Life and Start Over

So many times in my life, starting over was the only option. The death of my mother ... becoming homeless for a second time. Such experiences taught me how to start over in the struggle of life. Those are just a few examples. In those moments of starting over, I knew I would succeed. Years later ... I had the opportunity to experience the true meaning of living. For one month, I traveled to Asia, exploring the true meaning of life. After that month, I returned to working a 9-5, paying bills, and depression.

After experiencing what truly living and being free means to me, I'm now starting to exist again. This starting over has become painful and at times unbearable. How does one return to a life that no longer suits them? I ask this question on a daily basis. I wonder if I will ever experience truly living or if I'm destined for only existing? Each day I reminisce about my moments of living and traveling. Currently, I'm working on accepting my current position while working toward living again.

The "Start-Over Stories" Wrap-Up

We know that life will throw many things at us because it has a way of knocking people down. So, what do you do when it knocks you down? What do you do when you have nowhere else to go?

Honestly, I tried to figure out the answer to this question on my own and always failed to get it right. While I don't have the answer for you, I can tell you what I did.

I ran far away—to China. Heartbroken, depressed, and lost, I felt I had to remove myself from the situation. While this may sound like a bad thing, it was the best thing that could have happened to me. God knew that I would need a fresh start at this time in my life. It happened so fast, I couldn't believe it! While praying one day, I asked God to send me where he needed me to go. I had made a declaration that I wanted to be in his will and was tired of being disobedient. This was after I realized that everything I did up until that moment was from my flesh. My job, my relationship, where I lived. Everything! While I was comfortable teaching kindergarten and had convinced myself I was content being everyone's doormat, my spirit was tugging on me.

This experience was the best in my life. I grew a thicker skin and newfound confidence, and I fell back in love with myself. Some would say I was living my best life. This was my chance to reinvent myself and choose to do things that scared me. I went on dates, submerged my whole body in a pool (this is really a big deal!), rode rides I would have never dreamed of (an even bigger deal!), and most notably, I started writing this book.

One hot summer day, when two of my close "China friends" and I were on our way to see *The Bodyguard* on stage, I began to write down book ideas in my notes. The sixth and final one was "How Did I Start Over?" I began to think about the many ways people could start over. I asked my friends about my ideas, and we talked through the many ways people can start over.

A simple book title turned into a huge process, which would change my life forever and impact people across the world. As I stated earlier in the book, every passage you read in this book is real. That's what makes it so wonderful!

All of these narratives drew different conclusions to the question I've been asking myself for the past two years. Before I ever thought of this book. I wanted to start over but didn't know-how. I felt consumed by all of my situations. I was too comfortable to realize that God was about to flip my whole life upside down just to place it right-side-up again.

If you're still lost at this point, let me offer you some advice (although you didn't ask for it).

Try praying . . .

If you ask my friends, they will tell you that besides writing and teaching, I love to pray. I believe it unlocks the doors to any questions you may have. Sit and have some quiet time with God so he can direct you.

While I was away I would pray in my apartment. One day, God spoke to me and told me to go find a mat to pray on. I went to the store and found a brown mat that was big enough for me to sit or lay prostrate on. I sat and cried and prayed on it. I praised and worshiped on it. I received so much peace during the times I would sit on my mat and seek God.

What better way to start over than with God!

I also wrote in my journal, praying to God before or after work. While I wasn't perfect, it did help me clear my brain from thoughts that were crowding my space.

Remember these are just suggestions!

Just in case you would like to try it out, the back of this book will have space for you to write on your own. Write your own journey if you are starting over or have started over in the past.

If you believe that you have never had a time in your life that you have had to start over or begin again, well, honey, just keep on living! Next, you can write to God or to yourself. Use this space to journal and free your brain, allowing God to help you through whatever stage you are in your life.

Remember: it starts with you! You *can* start over, and you *will* be victorious just like all of the people in this book!

The Journey Starts Here . . .

Own your truth and write it out . . .

_____

_____

_____

_____

Be unapologetically you . . .

_____

_____

_____

_____

_____

_____

_____

_____

The journey may be rough, but the results will be amazing!

You deserve the elevation that will come after the storm . . .

Always believe in your ability to start over again!

Dear Lord,

Thank you for being the head of our lives. We trust you and believe that you have a plan for our lives. We know that sometimes, we have to go on unexpected paths, and it can discourage us, but we serve a father who died for us and who knows the plan for our lives. We thank you for forming us in our mother's wombs and giving us all a special assignment in this world. No matter who we are, where we come from, or what we've done, we are loved by you, Father.

Your love means so much to us. Lord, continue to comfort those people who are going through an uncomfortable stage in their lives. We ask that you send your peace and joy to overtake their sorrow. We know that you are just trying to elevate us and move us so that we can be used by you. Lord, continue to build rainbows in the clouds of life so the journey will be more bearable. Send your love, God.

We're so grateful for another chance to start over in you and for another chance to serve our purpose in the world. Bless every reader and their family.

In Jesus' name, Amen.

www.ingramcontent.com/pod-product-compliance
Lightning Source LLC
Chambersburg PA
CBHW051452290426
44109CB00016B/1729